PEOPLE IN THE NEWS

Kelly Clarkson

Music and Television Trailblazer

By Edna McPhee

Portions of this book originally appeared in *Kelly Clarkson* by Laurie Collier Hillstrom.

LUCENT PRESS

Published in 2020 by
Lucent Press, an Imprint of Greenhaven Publishing, LLC
353 3rd Avenue
Suite 255
New York, NY 10010

Designer: Deanna Paternostro
Editor: Molly Seeley

Cataloging-in-Publication Data

Names: McPhee, Edna.
Title: Kelly Clarkson: music and television trailblazer / Edna McPhee.
Description: New York : Lucent Press, 2020. | Series: People in the news | Includes index.
Identifiers: ISBN 9781534568341 (pbk.) | ISBN 9781534568358 (library bound) | ISBN 9781534568365 (ebook)
Subjects: LCSH: Clarkson, Kelly, 1982–Juvenile literature. | Singers–United States--Biography–Juvenile literature.
Classification: LCC ML3930.C523 M37 2020 | DDC 782.42164092 B–dc23

Printed in China

Contents

Foreword

We live in a world where the latest news is always available and where it seems we have unlimited access to the lives of the people in the news. Entire television networks are devoted to news about politics, sports, and entertainment. Social media has allowed people to have an unprecedented level of interaction with celebrities. We have more information at our fingertips than ever before. However, how much do we really know about the people we see on television news programs, social media feeds, and magazine covers?

Despite the constant stream of news, the full stories behind the lives of some of the world's most newsworthy men and women are often unknown. Who was Lady Gaga before she became a star? What does LeBron James do when he is not playing basketball? What inspires Lin-Manuel Miranda?

This series aims to answer questions like these about some of the biggest names in pop culture, sports, politics, and technology. While the subjects of this series come from all walks of life and areas of expertise, they share a common magnetism that has made them all captivating figures in the public eye. They have shaped the world in some unique way, and—in many cases—they are poised to continue to shape the world for many years to come.

These biographies are not just a collection of basic facts. They tell compelling stories that show how each figure grew to become a powerful public personality. Each book aims to paint a complete, realistic picture of its subject—from the challenges they overcame to the controversies they caused. In doing so, each book reinforces the idea that even the most famous faces on the news are real people who are much more complex than we are often shown in brief video clips or sound bites. Readers are also reminded that there is even more to a person than what they present to the world through social media posts, press releases, and interviews. The whole story of a person's life can only be discovered by digging beneath the surface of their public persona, and that is what this series allows readers to do.

The books in this series are filled with enlightening quotes from speeches and interviews given by the subjects, as well as quotes and anecdotes from those who know their story best: family, friends, coaches, and colleagues. All quotes are noted to provide guidance for further research. Detailed lists of additional resources are also included, as are timelines, indexes, and unique photographs. These text features come together to enhance the reading experience and encourage readers to dive deeper into the stories of these influential men and women.

Fame can be fleeting, but the subjects featured in this series have real staying power. They have fundamentally impacted their respective fields and have achieved great success through hard work and true talent. They are men and women defined by their accomplishments, and they are often seen as role models for the next generation. They have left their mark on the world in a major way, and their stories are meant to inspire readers to leave their mark, too.

Introduction

Kelly Clarkson: Pioneer

For many people, Kelly Clarkson will always be known as the first winner of the reality-TV singing competition *American Idol*. In 2002, during the show's premiere season, Clarkson captured the hearts of millions of television viewers with her powerful voice and appealing stage presence. Week after week, as some of her competitors' offerings failed to impress the judges and the American public, Clarkson gave strong performances that earned near-universal praise. On the final episode, with more than 22 million television viewers tuned in, she gained the grand prize of a million-dollar recording contract.

Because Clarkson's big break into the music business had such a dramatic, fairy-tale quality to it, many people (both within the music industry and outside it) wrote off Clarkson's journey as effortless. However, this shortchanges Clarkson's many setbacks—far from an overnight success, *American Idol* was only the most successful of a series of attempts by Clarkson to break into the music industry. Also, while part of Clarkson's winning charm on *American Idol* was due to her good-natured personality and laid-back energy, she would prove herself to be possessed of a mighty backbone borne of personal and professional struggle.

In many ways, *American Idol* proved to be a double-edged sword for Clarkson, whose connection to the show caused critics to question whether she won on the strength of her natural ability, or whether she owed her stardom to luck and effective marketing. During a whirlwind of interviews, promotional appearances, recording sessions, concert tours, and film shoots, Clarkson continually struggled to prove herself worthy of all the attention she received.

Clarkson has also faced an ongoing battle to be taken seriously within the recording industry. Not content to simply sing whatever guaranteed-hit, "pop factory" songs her label presented to her, Clarkson has shown a great deal of artistic ambition—she has always pressured recording executives to allow her to write her own songs and to take control over the direction of her career. However, even after her second album sold 6 million copies and won two Grammy Awards, Clarkson's desire to express herself and grow as an artist was still met with opposition from her record label. This led to a well-documented controversy over the content of her third album in 2007.

Though many *American Idol* winners have sought afterward to distance themselves from their origin story, Clarkson has remained a vocal supporter of the exposure and opportunity that the show gave her. "People have the wrong idea, like I don't want to talk about it," she has said. "I think it's a great thing. It was obviously the best way for me to come into the business and it's just a great opportunity for everyday normal people. It's like a Cinderella story every day."[1]

On the other hand, Clarkson recognizes that her association with the show has often made it difficult for her to be taken seriously as an artist. She has worked relentlessly to build a post-*Idol* career that is based on her artistic talent, hard work, and thoughtful career moves. A musician's success is often dependent on how they handle life as a celebrity, and Clarkson has at times struggled to navigate these waters.

"Fame is exactly what I thought it would be. It's hard and a lot of sacrifices," she explained. "If I could do without the fame part of it, I think I would. Basically I'm here for the fans and here for my music."[2]

Kelly Clarkson started her career by winning *American Idol* but would go on to prove that she was much more than the winner of a talent competition.

In the years that followed her appearance on *American Idol*, Clarkson has earned the respect of many fans, critics, and people in the recording industry for her determination to stand up for herself and to chart the course of her own career. Like all trailblazers, Clarkson has paved the way for female artists coming after her to have an easier road—but she herself was often put on the ropes as she sought to be given power over her career and her music.

"Back in the day, female artists were told to perform and then go sit in the corner," said country music legend Reba McEntire. "Thank God for people like [country music legend and successful businesswoman] Dolly Parton who took charge. Kelly is the same way. She knows what she wants. She's had a rough go of it in the music business. People think she just won *Idol* and everything else was easy. Not so. She's had to fight."[3]

However, Clarkson's drive, ambition, and independent spirit have helped her to achieve success on her own professional, artistic, and personal terms.

Chapter One

Small-Town Girl, Big-Time Dreams

Much of Kelly Clarkson's steel backbone and relentless determination can be credited to the struggles she faced in her upbringing. Her parents' tough divorce and the ensuing splintering of her family forced her to mature quickly, and the small Texas town she grew up in fostered in her a sense of self-reliance and independence. Although these traits were hard-won through hard times, they would become instrumental in Clarkson's later success.

A Splintered Family

Kelly Brianne Clarkson was born on April 24, 1982, in Fort Worth, Texas. Her mother, Jeanne Ann Rose, was an elementary school teacher, while her father, Stephen Michael Clarkson, worked as an engineer and car salesman. When Kelly was six years old, her parents divorced after seventeen years of marriage. The divorce divided Kelly's family, and she learned quickly that she needed to become her own advocate.

After the divorce, Kelly's older brother, Jason, remained with their father, who moved to Anaheim, California. Her older sister, Alyssa, went to live with an aunt. Only Kelly remained with their mother. Over the next few years, Kelly and her

Kelly Clarkson is shown here with her mother.

mother moved several times within Texas. Kelly missed her father and her brother and sister, and she found it difficult to adjust to new schools and different neighborhoods. In addition, mother and daughter faced financial troubles that weighed heavily on their lives.

Kelly's life became more stable and secure when her mother remarried, and the new family settled in Burleson, Texas, very near to Fort Worth. Kelly's family grew to include a stepfather, building contractor Jimmy Taylor, and five older stepsiblings at this time.

Heart of a Performer

Despite the difficulties she faced as a child, Kelly was a friendly, outgoing girl who loved to be the center of attention. "I've never really been insecure. I just skipped that. I've never been shy,"[4] she noted. Clarkson has credited her upbringing in Texas with her natural tendency toward friendliness; the culture of the place and the family she grew up in was one of neighborly openness, and she brought that gregarious nature with her as she grew up and grew out of her small-town roots.

Kelly had the heart of a performer and loved to entertain people from an early age, and she persuaded several of her childhood friends to play along with her favorite games. One of her friends, Ashley Donovan, kept a karaoke machine in her closet and put a sign on the door that read "Kelly's Recording Studio." Kelly spent a great deal of time in the closet, belting out popular songs while Ashley sat by listening.

Kelly also loved to sing the songs from Disney musicals such as *Beauty and the Beast*

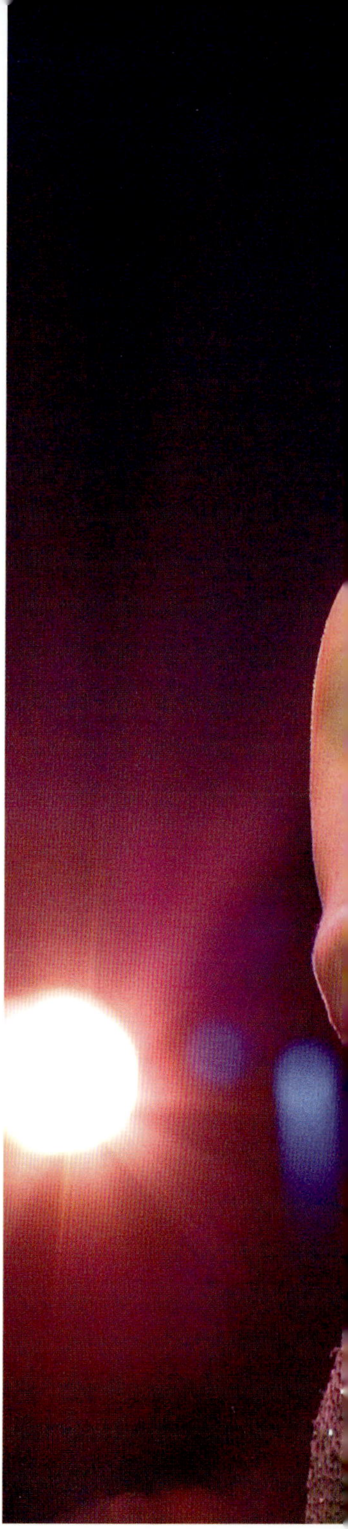

One of Clarkson's favorite parts of being a musician is performing. She is known as being a great performer who puts on memorable live shows.

and *The Little Mermaid* for her friends and family. Kelly and another childhood friend often produced their own shows in the living room. "Me and my friend Amber Gibson, when I was little, used to make up dances every hour," she remembered. "And we'd be like, 'OK, Mom, you have to watch,' and we'd drag people into the living room to be our audience. I never really thought about whether they liked it; I just wanted them to watch."[5]

Finding Confidence in Music

In 1995, Kelly was given an opportunity to perform beyond her family's living room. Cindy Glenn, a music teacher at Pauline Hughes Middle School, heard Kelly singing in the hallway. Recognizing the seventh grader's natural talent, Glenn invited her to join the school choir. Although Kelly had never taken singing lessons, she demonstrated a remarkable vocal range. She could move easily from singing low notes to high notes and back again, and she could adapt her voice to a wide variety of musical styles. Although this ability is something that many singers have to practice and work hard to perfect, it came naturally to Kelly.

Shortly after joining the choir, she was asked to perform a solo at a school assembly. She sang "Vision of Love"—a song made famous by pop star Mariah Carey—and received a standing ovation. From that moment on, Kelly knew that she wanted to become a professional singer. "Singing gave me confidence," she said. She added,

> *Friends at school were nervous because they didn't know what they wanted to do with the rest of their lives, but I had a peaceful feeling inside because I knew. I knew that I would make a living at this since a seventh-grade assembly, when I was about to go out and sing a Mariah Carey song in front of the whole town ... Singing just seemed a natural thing.*[6]

After her success at the junior high assembly, Kelly continued to sing in the choir as a student at Burleson High School. She also played on the varsity volleyball team and starred in several school musicals, including *Seven Brides for Seven Brothers* and *Brigadoon*. After graduating from high school in 2000, Kelly decided not to go to college. Although it was a big risk, she was determined to follow her dream of becoming a professional singer and did not see college as the best route to get there. Kelly's mom supported her dream and encouraged her to pursue music despite the risks of missing out on a college education.

An Ocean of Doubt

Although she enjoyed performing from an early age, Kelly did not always dream of becoming a professional musician. In fact, her first career goal was to study and care for sea creatures as a marine biologist. This childhood ambition ended in a hurry, however, when Kelly saw the movie *Jaws*. This blockbuster hit from 1975 features a great white shark that terrorizes the residents of a New England resort town. "I did really want to become a marine biologist, but then I saw *Jaws*, and had second thoughts," she recalled. "I remember someone telling me that sharks only attack in their own territory, and I thought to myself, 'Yeah, like the water!' and I left that dream right there!"[1]

1. Quoted in Terrina Hussein, "From Country Girl to Pop Star," Asia Africa Intelligence Wire, February 19, 2005.

Looking for a Chance

After graduating from high school, Kelly spent the next two years struggling to break into the music business. She wrote original songs and recorded herself singing them. She sent these demo tapes off to record companies in the hope of being discovered.

"I was sending out demos, getting doors slammed in my face,"[7] she recalled. It is incredibly difficult to get noticed in an industry crowded with talented individuals who all want the same thing, and Kelly made little headway at first. However, the support of her family and friends kept her from feeling discouraged.

Kelly's talent attracted some attention from recording industry executives. In fact, she received two offers of recording contracts. However, in both cases, Kelly turned the offers down because the record companies wanted to make fundamental changes to her style, not just in terms of the music she was making but in how she looked and behaved. Kelly knew who she was and who she was not, and she decided to hold out for a contract that recognized and celebrated the artist she was naturally. She was "confident enough that something better would come along."[8]

While she was trying to build a career as a singer, Kelly supported herself by taking a series of odd jobs in her hometown. She worked as a cocktail waitress at a local comedy club, as a clerk in a bookstore and in a pharmacy, and as a ticket seller in a movie theater. Through hard work and determination, Kelly eventually saved enough money to help her to follow her dream to Los Angeles, California—the heart of the American entertainment industry.

Learning from Failure

In late 2001, Kelly Clarkson moved to Los Angeles, hoping to meet and impress influential people in the entertainment industry. She lived with a friend in a small rental apartment off Melrose Avenue. For the next four months, Clarkson went to auditions for both singing jobs and acting roles. No stranger to the hustle of hard work, Clarkson was willing to take any opportunity to appear in front of a live audience and begin to make a name for herself in show business.

One of Clarkson's first professional appearances came when she was hired as an extra for the ABC-TV series *Sabrina, the Teenage Witch*. Clarkson was paid about $70 per day to be one of the people in the background in scenes where the main characters went out in public. She took several jobs like this, landing background rolls on programs like *That '70s Show* and *Dharma & Greg*. However, none of them led to any lasting connections or notable success.

Willing to try any avenue, Clarkson also auditioned for roles as a backup singer for various recording artists. She found these experiences frustrating and disappointing. Although several producers expressed appreciation for her strong voice, they all rejected her because they did not like her singing style or her appearance. The music industry can be a notoriously harsh, often prejudiced place, and Clarkson found this to be true: She was told that she needed to lose weight and that her soulful voice would not be successful with white audiences. Clarkson wanted to make art, but she found herself at the mercy of an industry that wanted to generate celebrity.

Then, a spark of hope: Clarkson began working with the well-known songwriter Gerry Goffin. During the 1960s and 1970s, Goffin had collaborated with singer Carole King to write hit songs such as "(You Make Me Feel Like) A Natural Woman" and "Up on the Roof." Goffin told Clarkson he was planning to record an album of new songs and wanted to feature her as a backup singer. Although the association with Goffin gave Clarkson some valuable on-the-job training in songwriting and recording techniques, the project was put on hold when Goffin developed a serious illness, and Clarkson was once again out of a job.

The Sting of Defeat

As if losing her best hope for success in the Goffin project was not enough, Clarkson suffered another blow: Her apartment in Los Angeles burned down, destroying everything. Though she hung around for a few more days, trying to make life work by sleeping in her car and showering at the gym, she quickly realized that this was not a sustainable way of living. She was not finding the artistic or professional fulfilment she had hoped for in the city of angels, and she was rapidly running out of money. Feeling let down by the industry, distraught at her personal losses, and exhausted from disappointment, Clarkson headed home to Texas.

Although her failure in Los Angeles was a major setback, Clarkson did not give up on her dream. She buckled down to pay the bills, working as a promoter for the energy drink Red Bull by driving a car with a giant can of Red Bull on top and handing out free samples at local bars, but this was just a way for her to stay afloat while she considered her next move. Los Angeles had not paved the way to stardom, but Clarkson knew that if she was persistent, she would find another route.

Clarkson worked as a promoter for Red Bull and drove a car that looked like those shown here.

Chapter Two

America's First Idol

By this point, Kelly Clarkson was used to disappointment. She had not been able to get any lasting acting jobs; her demos, while impressive, had not resulted in a worthwhile recording contract; and she came back from her first foray into the music business with less than she left with after the fire at her apartment in Los Angeles. However, there was something big on the horizon for Kelly Clarkson, something that nobody else had ever done before.

She was about to become the very first *American Idol*.

The Power of Friendship

There are moments in everyone's life when they have to rely on friends and family for support to get them through hard times. This was as true for Kelly Clarkson as it was for anybody else, and in the spring of 2002, she leaned on her network of loved ones as she regrouped from her failure in Los Angeles. Luckily, she had a lot of people who believed in her drive and her talent, and soon enough, this belief yielded concrete results.

Just a few days after she got back to Burleson, Clarkson went to visit her friends Jessica and Halie Brake. Their

None of the contestants knew what they were in for when they auditioned for *American Idol*, but it would change their lives.

mother, Terry, had heard an advertisement on the radio inviting singers to audition for spots on an upcoming television program. Terry showed the young women an internet site describing the new program, which was called *American Idol: The Search for a Superstar*. The auditions were being held in several cities across the United States, including nearby Dallas, Texas.

Knowing that Kelly had a powerful singing voice, the Brakes encouraged her to attend the auditions. "We always knew she could sing," Terry noted. "We just didn't know how or where she'd get the big chance."[9] When Kelly expressed doubts about the idea—claiming that she was not pretty enough or thin enough to win a televised singing competition—the Brakes convinced her to take a chance. "We told her, 'Just be yourself. If you show you're kind of silly and sweet, they'll love you,'"[10] Halie recalled. Jessica even filled out the online application for Kelly.

"Just a Girl with a Good Voice"

As the date of the audition approached, Clarkson grew more and more hopeful that it might provide a path to success in the music business. In fact, she became so excited about the audition that she could not sleep the night before. Always known for being a heavy sleeper, Clarkson did not want to risk oversleeping and missing her chance to appear on *American Idol*. Her solution to this problem was to stay up all night. She ended up going to the Brakes' house at four in the morning to seek her friends' help in staying awake.

When Clarkson showed up a few hours later at the Wyndham Anatole Hotel in Dallas, she joined thousands of other young singers who hoped to land a spot on the new reality TV series. *American Idol* was based on a hit British television program called *Pop Idol*. In both shows, amateur singers between the ages of 16 and 24 auditioned for a chance to showcase their talents on TV. After a series of callbacks and elimination rounds, the top 10 finalists were selected to appear on the show. These contestants sang songs in a different style each week, and their performances were reviewed by a panel of judges. At the end of each episode, TV viewers were asked to call in and vote for their favorite performers. The most popular contestants advanced to the next round, while the least popular were eliminated from the competition. At the end of the season, the overall winner received a million-dollar recording contract.

At the initial auditions for *American Idol*, Clarkson and the other hopefuls were each asked to sing a favorite song without accompaniment for 1 minute. Clarkson sang "At Last," a soulful ballad that was performed perhaps most famously by singer Etta James.

The three judges—British recording industry executive Simon Cowell, former pop singer Paula Abdul, and music producer Randy Jackson—praised her performance and voted unanimously to send her into the next round of the competition. Nevertheless, Cowell claimed that Clarkson's original audition was not particularly memorable. "There wasn't anything about her that jumped out at us at that point," he recalled. "She was just a girl with a good voice."[11]

Still, Clarkson did much better than most of the

Randy Jackson (left), Paula Abdul (center), and Simon Cowell (right) comprised the first judging panel for *American Idol*, though there have been many judges since.

10,000 people across the country who auditioned for the show. Although a few of the young singers stood out as talented performers, many other hopefuls sang painfully off-key and were ridiculed by the judges. Highlights from the early rounds of auditions, with their mix of impressive and terrible singers, became one of the most popular features of *American Idol*.

Trials of the Top 10

Following her original audition in Dallas, Clarkson was invited to a series of callbacks that narrowed the field of contestants to 120. These contestants were offered a trip to Hollywood, California, where they attended two more rounds of auditions. Clarkson continued to perform well, singing songs like Aretha Franklin's "Respect," Dionne Warwick's "I Say a Little Prayer," and Vanessa Williams's "Save the Best for Last." As more and more of the other singers were eliminated, Clarkson reached the top 30 finalists, who were given the opportunity to appear on television.

American Idol made its premiere on the Fox television network on June 11, 2002, and the show quickly became the surprise hit of the summer. Since there was only

Clarkson insists that there was no conflict or drama between the contestants during their time on the show.

time for 10 contestants to sing in each hour-long episode, Clarkson did not perform on the air until two weeks later. She decided to sing "Respect," the classic Motown tune that had helped make Aretha Franklin a superstar. "I wasn't on the first two shows and I thought I would have to come out with a big song," Clarkson explained. "I had sung 'Respect' karaoke with friends. I feel that song and I love that song. It's upbeat, it's got soul, it shows your range. It's a show-stopper, the song itself."[12]

Clarkson's version of "Respect" impressed both the judges and TV viewers. She was named one of the ten finalists who would compete to become the first *American Idol* winner. Clarkson and the other finalists then moved into a

Tough Love: Simon Cowell and the Idols

Simon Cowell, the acid-tongued British judge known for his blunt criticisms of contestants' performances, was one of the most popular aspects of the first seasons of *American Idol*. Known as "Mr. Nasty," Cowell felt no need to be kind with his criticisms; if he felt a competitor had not performed well, he told them so—often in sharp, sarcastic ways.

The son of a music executive, Cowell was born on October 7, 1959, in London, England. After dropping out of school when he was 17, Cowell took a job in the mailroom at EMI Music Publishing. He quickly moved up through the ranks and proved himself to be a good judge of singing talent. Cowell later moved to music giant BMG and set up his own record label, S Records, which signed up a number of well-known pop groups. In fact, between 1997 and 2002, Cowell's label was responsible for artists who sold more than 25 million thirteen-bedroom, eight-bathroom mansion on Mulholland Drive, overlooking Los Angeles. The luxurious estate featured a pool, hot tub, workout room, and chef. Unfortunately for Clarkson, her busy schedule of promotional appearances, rehearsals, voice coaching, and wardrobe selection left her very little time to enjoy her surroundings. "The stress level of learning songs and performing them live on television is huge," acknowledged *American Idol* executive producer Nigel Lythgoe. "Most artists never do that in a lifetime."[13]

Despite the grueling schedule and pressure-packed atmosphere of the competition, Clarkson claimed that she and the other finalists got along well during the taping of the show.

albums and produced 17 number one songs.

In 2001, Cowell joined forces with fellow entertainment executive Simon Fuller to create *Pop Idol*, a British TV show in which young, unknown singers competed to win a recording contract. Cowell appeared on the show as one of the judges and received a great deal of attention for his harsh criticisms of contestants' performances.

The following year, Cowell starred in the U.S. version of the show, *American Idol*. Adding to his reputation as one of television's favorite villains, he told various contestants that their singing was "pathetic" or "rubbish."

Cowell refused to apologize for his critical words, claiming that he was just doing his job. "My only objective is to find a great singer who is going to sell millions of records for my label," he explained in *People* magazine. "If you get called a few names, well—tough luck, you know? I'll live with that."[1]

1. Julie K. L. Dam and Alexis Chiu, "Judge Dread," *People*, July 8, 2002, p. 107.

"Of course, there are going to be ups and downs with people because of the stress, but nobody got in fights," she recalled. "We were all too busy. Nobody believes us, but we were literally too busy to have any kind of conflict."[14]

Spreading Her Wings

As the competition continued, Clarkson and the other finalists performed a new song each week. They chose most of the songs themselves, although sometimes their selection was limited by the theme assigned to an episode of the show. One week, the contestants had to sing Motown songs, for example, while other weeks featured love songs, big band tunes, or songs from a certain decade. Regardless of the theme, Clarkson consistently chose soulful ballads made famous by some of the most powerful voices in the music industry. She sang Diana Ross's "All I Need" for Motown week, Aretha Franklin's "(You Make Me Feel Like) A Natural Woman" for 1960s week, Dionne Warwick's "Walk on By" for love song week, and Celine Dion's "I Surrender" for 1980s/1990s week.

While most of the other finalists experienced ups and downs, Clarkson's performances were given mostly positive reviews from Cowell, Abdul, and Jackson. In fact, one writer claimed that the range and power of Clarkson's voice was "a constant source of awe to *Idol*'s trio of feuding judges"[15] throughout the competition. While her rivals were being eliminated one by one, Clarkson remained humble about her talent. "I know my voice and what I can do," she stated. "I just rehearse and pray to God that He won't let me screw up on national television."[16]

Clarkson quickly became a fan favorite. One fan even took the opportunity to kiss her hand during a live broadcast.

Along with her impressive voice, Clarkson's friendly, down-to-earth personality was popular with fans of the show. She seemed charming and bubbly on camera, as likable for her big personality as her big voice. She drew people into the fun with her performances. As a reviewer who watched the taping of an episode with a live audience noted,

> *Of all the contestants, Clarkson seemed to be enjoying herself the most. Her talent is natural and she has fun, a highly underrated quality. The power of her voice sent chills, and … it felt like everyone, as if they were sitting in a bar, wanted to sing along with her.*[17]

One Voice, Three Judges

During the first season of *American Idol*, the show's three judges—Paula Abdul, Simon Cowell, and Randy Jackson—received nearly as much public interest and media attention as the contestants. Each week, fans and reviewers analyzed the judges' comments, compared their styles and preferences, and shared information about their backgrounds and personalities. "Abdul tends to give out warm fuzzies; Jackson is hit-or-miss in giving a direct assessment but generally forgiving of minor slips; Cowell tells it like it is,"[1] Phil Gallo wrote in *Daily Variety*.

Immediately after Clarkson's victory on *American Idol*, many interviewers asked for her opinions about the judges. They were particularly interested to hear what she had to say about Simon Cowell, the British recording executive whose harsh criticism sometimes brought contestants to the verge of tears. "Simon

In Los Angeles, Clarkson had been told by producers and executives that to succeed she would need to change her look and her musical style, but on *Idol*, she expressed herself as she was rather than as people may have wanted her to be. This loyalty to her own sense of self-expression helped Clarkson stand out on the show, where many other contestants tried to stand out with their fashion choices rather than their musical talent.

Making the Cut

By mid-August, six of the ten finalists had been eliminated from *American Idol*, leaving only Clarkson, Tamyra Gray, Justin Guarini, and Nikki McKibbin to compete for the grand prize.

fills his purpose," she told the *Sunday Mirror*. "He informs the performers and the audience at home that the music industry is tough and not everyone will love you. He gives it to you straight. Sometimes he's wrong—like all critics—but he's so charming and clever he makes it acceptable."[2]

Although Clarkson enjoyed working with singer and choreographer Paula Abdul, she admitted that Randy Jackson was her favorite judge. She showed respect for his range of experiences in the music industry as a bass player and record producer.

Throughout the competition, Clarkson always tried to remain calm and avoid getting too excited, or too disappointed, by the judges' comments by reminding herself that they were just three people's opinions, and not necessarily a reflection of her real value.

1. Phil Gallo, "*American Idol*: The Search for a Superstar," *Daily Variety*, August 20, 2002, p. 5.

2. "Fashion: An American Life; In the U.S., *American Idol* Winner Kelly Clarkson Is a Diva in the Making," *Sunday Mirror*, September 7, 2003, p. 14.

Many people predicted that the competition would come down to Clarkson and Gray, who were widely considered to have the strongest voices among the remaining contestants. Gray was clearly Cowell's favorite. He and millions of television viewers were shocked, therefore, when Gray became the next contestant to be eliminated.

The following week, the top three contestants each sang two songs that were selected by the judges. Clarkson sang Celine Dion's "Think Twice" and Mariah Carey's "Without You." Once again, her performances wowed the judges, and she advanced to the final round. McKibbin ended up being eliminated on the basis of viewer votes, so Clarkson faced off against Guarini in the season finale. Despite the pressure of performing in the finale, Clarkson insisted that she felt no animosity toward her rival because she did not view it as a competition between the two of them. Kelly Clarkson was competing against herself, trying to get better every week.

As the season finale of *American Idol* approached, most people argued that Clarkson had a stronger singing voice than her rival. Still, few people were willing to count Guarini out. The curly-haired native of Doylestown, Pennsylvania, had a strong stage presence, and his good looks and pleasant manner had helped him develop a large fan base among young female viewers of the show. "Justin Guarini definitely has the 'X' factor," noted one reviewer. "Sexy and smooth, he [comes] across as the real deal."[18]

An Idol at Last

The final performance demanded that both Clarkson and Guarini perform three songs, two of which had been written specifically for the show: "A Moment Like This" and "Before Your Love." They sang back-to-back so that audiences could see the different ways that both musicians interpreted the music and to eliminate the possibility that one of the contestants was judged on song choice rather than talent.

For their third song, the finalists were allowed to pick from their previous performances. Guarini sang "Get Here," to applause; Clarkson went back to the song that had started everything for her—"Respect." As she said before, the song allowed her to display her range, to get into a groove, and to show emotion. TV viewers were then allowed to vote for their favorite performer, and votes were tallied immediately afterward, though the winner would not be announced until the following night.

On September 4, 2002, nearly 23 million people across the country tuned in to the 2-hour special episode to find out who would win the very first season of *American Idol*. The final tally was exceptionally close, but Clarkson edged out Guarini with 58 percent of the 15.5 million votes cast. The contestants showed no bad blood between them; Guarini hugged Clarkson and praised her talent afterward.

When she heard the results, a delighted Clarkson cried tears of joy. The tears continued streaming down her face as she performed the inspirational ballad that had been written for the winner of the show, "A Moment Like This." The other nine finalists eventually joined her on stage to help her finish the song. Clarkson found the whole experience a bit overwhelming. "I was so exhausted from the competition I didn't know I was crying until I watched a tape of the final show a few weeks later," she recalled. "Isn't that funny? I don't remember a bit of it."[19]

"A Moment Like This" was written for the winner of *American Idol* and would become Clarkson's first number one hit.

American Idol
American Idol

Chapter Three

The Struggles of Success

Winning *American Idol* changed Kelly Clarkson's life completely. No longer just a girl with a good voice, she had become an American sensation, and everybody wanted a piece of her success. Sucked into a whirlwind of publicity and appearances, Clarkson was thrilled to have finally achieved her dream—but there were downsides to fame and success, and she was about to find out that making it to the top was just the beginning of the fight.

Record-Shattering Success

Clarkson auditioned for *American Idol* hoping for exposure, but as the winner, she had also earned the grand prize of a million-dollar recording contract with RCA Records. Her first single release—featuring the two songs that were written especially for the show, "A Moment Like This" and "Before Your Love"—came out on September 17, 2002. After making its debut at number 52 on *Billboard* magazine's Top 100 chart, it sold a remarkable 236,000 copies in its first week of release, jumping all the way to the number one spot. With this, Clarkson broke a longstanding record—one that had been set by the Beatles—for the biggest jump in Billboard chart history.

Clarkson's commitments to the *American Idol* production team did not end with her victory. In the weeks following her victory on *American Idol*, she was required to make many public appearances, with the aim of generating sales of her single and increasing interest in future seasons of *American Idol*. As a result, Clarkson performed songs on a number of TV talk shows and gave several interviews on the radio. She was also featured in countless articles in newspapers across the country, and her image graced the covers of several major magazines. The cable TV music channel VH-1 even produced a documentary about her life.

In fact, for many months after the show wrapped, Clarkson remained very involved with the television show that had launched her career. Eager to capitalize on both Clarkson's and *Idol*'s success, the Fox network televised a concert special featuring Clarkson and the other 29 finalists. A few weeks later, Clarkson's music video for "A Moment Like This" made its debut on the cable music channel MTV. Filmed in an old, abandoned theater, the video also featured footage of Clarkson's emotional victory on *American Idol*.

Clarkson's hectic schedule continued in October, when she embarked on a six-week, thirty-city national concert tour with the top ten *Idol* contestants. She also sang four songs on *American Idol Greatest Moments*, a compilation CD of music by the show's ten finalists. In addition to the two tracks from her single, Clarkson also performed "Respect" and "(You Make Me Feel Like) A Natural Woman." She also joined the rest of the finalists in a group rendition of "California Dreamin'."

The Flip Side of Fame

Although Clarkson's record-breaking single sales and hectic publicity schedule made lots of headlines in the fall of 2002, many people in the entertainment industry expected her fame

A History of "Respect"

Kelly Clarkson distinguished herself from the competition on *American Idol* by singing "Respect," a rock-and-roll classic with a powerful message. *Detroit Free Press* music writer Kelley L. Carter described the song as a powerfully influential part of the history of pop music.

When Clarkson performed "Respect" during her first appearance on *American Idol*, it earned her a spot in the top 10. She sang the song again during the finals, and it helped her defeat rival Justin Guarini to win the million-dollar recording contract. Clarkson explained that she had always appreciated the spirit of the song, as well as its influential place in music history.

Written by Otis Redding in 1965, "Respect" became famous two years later, when Motown legend Aretha Franklin recorded her own funky, aggressive version. Franklin's single came out in June 1967, a time when African Americans were demanding equal rights and opportunities in society through the civil rights movement. That summer, in fact, civil rights protests and violent race riots took place in Detroit and other cities across the United States.

Against this historical backdrop, many people came to associate "Respect" with the African American struggle for civil rights. "When Aretha came out with 'Respect,' we weren't getting any respect. Black folks were being disrespected, being beat down, killed trying to get the right to vote," remembered civil rights leader Benjamin Chavis. "So when she came out with this song, 'Respect,' it was like she was fulfilling not only an urgency of the movement of that time, but she made known through her song that we were going to get respect."[1]

1. Quoted in Kelley L. Carter, "Aretha Franklin's 'Respect': How Sassy Song Became Anthem for an Era,'" *Detroit Free Press*, August 30, 2018, www.freep.com/story/entertainment/music/aretha-franklin/2018/08/30/aretha-franklin-songs-respect/1133856002/.

After winning *Idol*, Clarkson still had obligations to promote the show and did a series of interviews and media appearances, including this one with Jay Leno.

to be short-lived. They thought that the popularity of *American Idol* would fade quickly from the public eye and that Clarkson's singing career would be over as quickly as it had begun. After all, reality-based television programs like *Survivor*, *The Bachelor*, and *The Amazing Race* had already turned dozens of ordinary Americans into instant celebrities, but at that point, none of those people had managed to turn their success on reality TV into a lasting career.

On the other hand, some analysts claimed that *American Idol* had more in common with the talent shows that were popular in the early decades of TV history than with modern reality TV programs. "For the most part, we have always had some original amateur hour. It has always been a viable format for Americans. It's just a matter of adapting it for the times,"[20] said Ron Simon, curator of the Museum of Radio and Records. These TV and radio shows produced a number of singers who went on to become big stars, including Frank Sinatra and Gladys Knight.

Despite these historical examples, some people in the music industry rejected Clarkson's talent simply because it was discovered on *American Idol*. They believed that her popularity stemmed from her association with the show, rather than from her artistic gifts. Some felt that Clarkson did not have the artistic chops of her peers. "For many in the music business, *Idol* is the starkest example of how marketing concepts seem to have trumped art," noted one critic. "Some analysts have said the show's appeal stems more from the drama of competition and the judges' critiques than it does from the music."[21]

Much of the criticism Clarkson faced immediately following her victory centered around her top-selling single. Many critics attributed the popularity of the recording to its connection with the TV show. They claimed that "A Moment Like This" and "Before Your Love"—despite all of the national radio airplay they received—were inferior songs that were not well suited to Clarkson's voice. They warned that she and her managers needed to come up with significantly better material for her first album. "Celine Dion or Mariah Carey wouldn't cross the street to spit on those songs. And that's who Clarkson is competing against now—it's not just Justin anymore," wrote *Rolling Stone* music editor Joe Levy. "People voted for Kelly because she had a sweetness and a vulnerability in addition to astounding ability. They've got to give her songs that communicate something about her personality. Otherwise, she might well be queen of the Thanksgiving Day parade rather than a pop star."[22]

America has a long history of talent competitions. Famous artists like Gladys Knight (pictured above) were discovered that way.

In Her Own Defense

Clarkson heard these criticisms, and in some cases, she understood or even agreed with them; she admitted that "A Moment Like This" was written to suit *American Idol*'s finale and that it was not her preferred style of music. However, to Clarkson, that this somehow meant that she did not have what it took to be a singer seemed completely disconnected; she insisted that she and the other contestants had showcased their individual abilities and personalities on the program. She argued that TV viewers had chosen her as the winner of the competition on the basis of her artistic performances, which was what all aspiring musicians go through. It may be that Clarkson's gigs were on national television, rather than in bars or small concert venues, but she still performed, and her audience grew based on those performances.

She also emphasized that she—rather than the show's producers—had been responsible for those performances by making all of the important decisions regarding songs, arrangements, and wardrobe. "There are going to be people, until the day I die, who are going to say, 'Oh, she's the product of a TV show.' To some extent that's true. On the other hand, we made the show—so who's the product?" she noted. "It's funny to me whenever people use the words 'puppet' and 'manufactured.' It's the exact opposite. I went on the show. I sang what I wanted. I wore what I wanted. I said what I wanted."[23]

Clarkson ultimately chose to ignore the critics who questioned whether winning a TV singing competition would provide her with a path to lasting stardom. She was thrilled to have finally gotten her big break, and she was determined to make the most of the opportunity. "Any artist is going to accept whatever comes their way," she declared. "They're not going to say, 'No way, I'm not going to go on this hit television show. I want to go the hard route.'"[24]

Clarkson recognized that the fame she had gained as the winner of *American Idol* would not last long unless she continued to work hard. Although the show had provided her with a great deal of exposure and garnered her a great deal of fans, she knew that what *Idol* had really given her was the opportunity to build a lasting career—not the guarantee of one. Rather than riding the wave of fame, Clarkson buckled down and decided to use this chance to keep growing, professionally and artistically. "She never once had to be told that she was going to have to keep waking up every day and proving herself," said an RCA executive. "Despite all of her sudden fame, she knew what it took to break a record and establish a career: not just one television show, but constant promotion and constant performing."[25]

Creative Control

During all this publicity and media attention, Clarkson started working on her debut album. Executives at RCA Records pushed her to finish the recording sessions very quickly. They wanted to release the CD in November 2002 to take advantage of her popularity and to increase record sales at Christmas. "Performers who appeal to that teenage demographic can come and go so rapidly," concert promoter Jerry Thompson explained. "That demographic just turns on to its likes and dislikes a day at a time."[26]

Representatives of the record label believed that timing would be an important factor in the album's success, so they recruited a number of well-known songwriters to quickly supply material for it. They also arranged for Clarkson to work with Clive Davis, a legendary record producer and the head of RCA Records.

Shortly after beginning work on the album, Clarkson asked Davis to let her record some of the songs she had written over the years. She felt that the album would only reflect her personality, interests, and musical style if she were allowed to contribute original songs to it. Once again, her confidence in herself and in her talent helped her stay the course when it would have been easy to give in to the pressure around her. "I'm all about my sound and my style," she stated. "That's important for me to stand up to. I came out on the show being myself and doing what I like, and people voted for me. So I already have a fan base based on what I like and what I do."[27]

Unfortunately for Clarkson, Davis and other RCA executives

resisted the idea of letting her write songs for the album. They argued that Clarkson had won over fans by using her powerful voice to interpret the work of other artists. Since she had never demonstrated her talents as a songwriter, they wanted established musicians to compose the songs for her first album. However, Clarkson was determined to make an album that reflected her unique talents and tastes, even if it meant delaying the CD's release by several months. "Basically people right off the show said, 'Of course her CD is gonna do good. She's got to strike while the iron is hot,'" she recalled. "I put my foot down and said, 'Nope, not gonna do that.' ... I wanted to make a CD that was a representation of me, not a representation of the show."[28]

Clarkson and RCA eventually reached a compromise that gave her more time to create the album that she wanted. After sitting down with *American Idol* producer Simon Fuller, Clarkson argued her case successfully enough that RCA agreed to wait until the spring of 2003. Although she would not be writing her own songs for the album, she was able to choose the songs that she felt were the most representative of who she was and what she liked, and this compromise worked both for the producers putting the album together and the artist who would be responsible for singing them. It was Clarkson's first big battle for her artistic integrity, and although it would not be her last, it taught her an important lesson about putting her foot down when it mattered, no matter how powerful her opponents were.

"Miss Independent"

Clarkson's decision to delay the release of her debut album until she could find songs that suited her musical style proved to be a good one. While she continued to work on the CD, Clarkson released a second single, "Miss Independent," that marked a major musical departure from the ballads on her previous release. Clarkson wanted to prove that she was not a one-note performer; although she had won *Idol* on the strength of her ballads, she had many more creative sides to her. "I was the one who pushed the single," she explained. "I need people to know right away that I

Clarkson's look for "Miss Independent" mirrored the song's attitude: She appeared fierce and strong, and she made it known that she could stand on her own two feet. These characteristics would come into play many times over in Clarkson's career.

like rock, soul, groove, country, urban … I don't want everyone to think my album is a bunch of ballads."[29]

"Miss Independent" was originally written by Christina Aguilera, but the pop star had left the song unfinished when it did not fit on one of her albums. Clarkson collaborated with veteran songwriter Rhett Lawrence to finish the song and adapt it to her personal style. The song's rock edge and assertive lyrics helped expand Clarkson's fan base beyond *American Idol* viewers and reached the top 10 on the Billboard charts. It also earned Clarkson a Grammy Award nomination for Best Female Pop Vocal Performance of the Year.

More Than Meets the Eye

The success of "Miss Independent"—as well as the contrast between its style and that of "A Moment Like This"—created a great deal of anticipation about the release of Clarkson's debut album. When *Thankful* finally came out in April 2003, it did not disappoint the singer's many fans. In addition to the tracks that had already been released as singles, the album included songs in a wide range of musical styles, from pop and rock to country and gospel. "I grew up with many different styles of music," Clarkson explained. "There's no way I'm going to limit myself … I like rock. I like alternative. I like country. I like R&B [rhythm and blues]. I am going to keep it pretty versatile."[30]

Although Clarkson was not credited with the solo writing of any of the album's songs, she collaborated with well-known songwriters on several of the tracks. For example, she co-wrote the title track, "Thankful," with R&B star Kenneth "Babyface" Edmonds. Clarkson said that she wrote the song as a way to express her appreciation to everyone who had supported her career. To her, the song was a gift to the people who had kept her going even when she had wanted to give up—her family and friends who had always believed in her and, in fact, had been the reason she had auditioned for *Idol* in the first place.

Despite concerns, delaying the release date of her debut album did not seem to have a negative impact on sales. *Thankful* sold an impressive 297,000 copies in its first week of release

Clarkson had a lot to be thankful for with the release of her first album, but she was already starting to feel constricted by her lack of creative control.

to debut at number one on the Billboard charts. It went on to sell over 2 million copies by the end of the year and was certified double platinum by the Recording Industry Association of America. One reviewer claimed that the delay actually made the album more appealing to fans because it gave Clarkson and Davis "time to figure out how to balance the expectations of people who wanted an *Idol* souvenir with those who demanded signs of artistic growth."[31]

Thankful received mostly favorable reviews from music critics. Many reviewers praised the power and range of Clarkson's voice. "Her voice, at times raspy, at times beautifully sultry, is a potent reminder of why America embraced her," Henry Goldblatt wrote in *Entertainment Weekly*. He added,

> *Clarkson glides through octaves with the masterful control of someone who's been doing this for decades. And her range is awesome: in a dozen tracks, she owns pop ("Just Missed the Train"), R&B ("Thankful"), country ("Low"), and gospel ("Anytime").*[32]

On the other hand, some critics felt that the songs on *Thankful* showed too much variety. They claimed that the broad range of musical styles on the album made it difficult to show Clarkson's real personality. Some critics thought she was trying to hedge her bets by imitating a handful of popular artists. What Clarkson had intended to be a showcase of her varied interests and talents was received by some as a case of trying to put something for everybody on the album, to appeal to the broadest possible audience.

Still, even those who had reservations about the album recognized her talent. No matter how they felt about the songs themselves, critics across the board praised her voice and the personality that came with it.

"It Was Going to Be Real, Real Bad"

While Clarkson's first album was given mostly positive reviews, most critics did not like her first movie role, which Clarkson agreed to not as an artistic choice but as part of a business deal Clarkson made following her victory on *American Idol*. She had agreed to co-star with Justin Guarini in a musical love story called *From Justin to Kelly*. *Idol* creator Simon Fuller rushed the movie through production to take advantage of the popularity the two young singers had gained from *American Idol*.

On-screen/Off-screen

From the time that Kelly Clarkson and Justin Guarini emerged as the two final contestants on *American Idol*, fans of both singers wondered about the nature of their personal relationship. Although each expressed fondness and respect for the other throughout the competition, they both insisted that they were just good friends. They also claimed that the show and its aftermath kept them far too busy to have time for a boyfriend or girlfriend.

Despite their protests, however, the tabloids remained full of rumors about a romance between the two singers once they wrapped up *American Idol*. Interest in the couple peaked during the filming of their romantic beach movie in the spring of 2003. Clarkson and Guarini were the center of a lot of celebrity gossip. "My mom called up and joked, 'I'm so mad I didn't get a wedding invitation!'"[1] Clarkson recalled.

The rumors finally started to die down after the movie came out and both singers moved on to other projects. However, in 2015, both Clarkson and Guarini confirmed that they had a brief fling after *American Idol* ended.

1. Jason Lynch, "From Idol to Star?," *People*, April 23, 2003, p. 71.

Though she had committed to the movie and knew she had to live up to her commitment, Clarkson knew that the script for *From Justin to Kelly* was bad.

The movie was filmed in Miami over six weeks and released in June 2003.

Clarkson had misgivings about the film from the beginning. She disliked the story—in which a girl from Texas meets and falls in love with a boy from Pennsylvania while on spring break in Florida—and also expressed doubts about her own acting ability. She had made it this far in her career by trusting her instincts and her talent, but this was an area where she simply did not know if she had any. She had not set out to get into the movie business, so this was a departure for the young star, and she knew even as she read the script that the film would be terrible. Speaking of the movie afterward, she admitted, "I knew when I read the script it was going to be real, real bad, but when I won, I signed that piece of paper, and I could not get out of it."[33]

Unfortunately for Clarkson, her predictions about the film's quality turned out to be true. *From Justin to Kelly* bombed at the box office, earning only $5 million—or less than half of what it had cost to make. It also received scathing reviews from movie critics, who complained about the predictable plot, silly song and dance routines, and poor acting performances. In a review for the *New York Times*, for example, Stephen Holden wrote that Clarkson and Guarini "go through their paces like dutiful puppets, lip-synching and strenuously aerobicizing in the beach party dance sequences to numbers that run from sanitized rap to the strawberry sundae froth of several billowing love songs."[34] Several internet polls ranked the movie among the worst films ever made.

From Justin to Kelly received so much bad press that some people worried it might harm Clarkson's singing career, which had looked so promising a few months earlier with the success of her first album. Clarkson kept her head up, viewed the situation with a sense of humor, and refused to allow one bad decision to define her career. She knew that over the course of any long career, there are ups and downs, and this would simply be a small blip in a big body of work.

World Idol

Up to this point, Clarkson's career had been closely tied to *American Idol*. She had done press tours, filmed a movie, contributed to the show's album, and was constantly being asked about and reminded of her time on the show. Although this did not bother her—it was, after all, *American Idol* that had given

Clarkson participated in *World Idol*, alongside the winners of the *Idol* franchise from various countries around the world.

her the opportunities she had been striving so hard for—she was about to embark on the next stage of her work.

Before she could, however, there was one more obligation, and in December 2003, she returned to the *Idol* universe as a contestant on *World Idol*, a spinoff competition that featured the winners of different national *Idol* programs. Clarkson, widely considered to be the favorite, went up against her peers from all over the world, singing "(You Make Me Feel Like) A Natural Woman" in the finals. Despite a strong performance, she finished in second place, behind Norwegian winner Kurt Nilsen.

With *World Idol* wrapped, Clarkson closed the book on the *Idol* chapter of her life. She had entered the competition hoping just to gain some exposure and instead came out the show's first winner. She had received a Grammy nomination and had a best-selling, critically successful album. She could not have known at this point that some of her greatest battles were still ahead—but still, she had come a long way from being just a girl with a nice voice from Texas.

Chapter Four

Taking a Risk

Though Kelly Clarkson would praise and express gratitude toward *American Idol* for the duration of her career, she knew it was time to turn over a new page. She wanted to grow as an artist, and that meant taking greater control of her music and her career. She had fulfilled her obligations to the show and wanted to use her second album, 2004's *Breakaway*, to write more of her own music and further develop her sound.

The Burden of Idol

The whirlwind of publicity that had followed Clarkson's victory on *American Idol* finally began to subside in late 2003. Many people within the music industry expressed admiration for the way in which Clarkson had handled her instant fame. Most people thought that she showed maturity in dealing with an intense, pressure-packed situation. "It's pretty heavy, what happened to her. She was thrown into the ocean without a life preserver," said Clarkson's mentor, country music legend Reba McEntire. "And she handled it. I don't know that I could have."[35]

Clarkson was determined to take greater control over the future direction of her career. While she appreciated the gifts given to her via her experience on *American Idol*, she felt that the time had come for her to begin distancing herself from the show. "I don't think I should hang onto the show, and I don't think the show should hang onto me,"[36] she explained. "The whole point of *American Idol* was for me to get a record deal and be able to make music that I love. People change and grow. My thing as an artist is to be limitless."[37]

Take a Chance, Make a Change

The experience of recording her first album gave Clarkson the confidence she needed to exert more control over her second album. "I had more experience being in a studio and working with major producers and writers and so on," she noted. "I kind of came in and knew exactly what I wanted to do. I got to pick people who I wanted to work with."[38]

As she began working on *Breakaway*, her follow-up album to *Thankful*, Clarkson's biggest priority was to write as many songs for the album as possible. Once again, however, she faced resistance from Simon Fuller and his company, 19 Entertainment. "To be totally honest, the problem was I wanted to write a lot of my own songs on *Breakaway*. Nobody else wanted me to. So there was this big ol' fight,"[39] Clarkson recalled. In order to get more creative control over the content of her second album, Clarkson ended her relationship with the management team that had guided her career since *American Idol*. Instead, she signed a contract with the Firm, a talent agency that represented many big names in the music business.

Breaking Away

Clarkson's new management team was more supportive of her desire to write songs for her second album. Clarkson worked on *Breakaway* through much of 2004. Although she continued to work with well-known songwriters—including Max Martin, who had composed hit songs for Britney Spears and the Backstreet Boys; John Shanks, who had written for

Breakaway would become one of Clarkson's most successful albums, but it was also the start of conflict between her and the executives at RCA.

Sheryl Crow and Alanis Morissette; and former Evanescence guitar player Ben Moody—Clarkson was credited with the songwriting on six of the album's tracks.

When Clarkson's second album was finally released in December 2004, it immediately shot up to the number three position on the Billboard album charts. It also received glowing reviews from music critics, many of whom felt that *Breakaway* compared favorably with *Thankful*. Several reviewers commented that the new album's rock-based sound seemed to reflect Clarkson's individual style more accurately. "This time, the Texas-born chanteuse digs deeper emotionally, and the songs … generally fit better with her upbeat, down-to-earth personality," wrote one critic. "Perhaps the greatest asset of

Clive Davis: The Legend Behind Legends

As the president of RCA Records, Clive Davis is one of the most powerful figures in the recording industry. Over the course of his 40-year career, he has become legendary for his ability to find and develop talented musicians.

Davis was born on April 4, 1932, in Brooklyn, New York. After graduating from New York University and Harvard Law School, he ended up working in the legal department of Columbia Records, a division of CBS. He loved the music industry and worked his way up to become president of Columbia Records in 1967.

In this position, Davis discovered and signed many newly emerging rock-and-roll artists. Some of the artists he introduced to American audiences include Janis Joplin, Santana, Bruce Springsteen, Chicago, and Pink

Breakaway—whose title track plays like Clarkson's anthem, about a small-town girl going for it—is that she sounds more like herself, which allows her to move beyond the typical."[40]

At the Top

Breakaway soon proved to be just as popular among radio listeners and record buyers as it was among critics. The album produced four singles that spent time at the top of the Billboard charts, including the huge hit "Since U Been Gone." In a review for *Billboard*, Chuck Taylor described the song as "an utterly ideal showcase for Clarkson. There's glorious tempo, enough edge to rattle the speakers, a relentless,

Floyd. Although Davis doubled Columbia's market share within three years, he was fired in 1972 following a government investigation into the company's finances.

After leaving Columbia, Davis merged various record labels to form Arista Records. At Arista, Davis guided the careers of a range of talented musicians, including Whitney Houston, Aretha Franklin, Annie Lennox, Sean "Diddy" Combs, and the Grateful Dead.

Following a series of disagreements with parent company BMG, he left the company in 2000. That same year, Davis joined the Rock and Roll Hall of Fame as a record producer.

In 2003, Davis became the head of RCA Records, the company that provided recording contracts to *American Idol* winners. He took an active role in guiding Kelly Clarkson's early career and won a Grammy Award for his work as producer of her second album, *Breakaway*. However, Davis and Clarkson publicly disagreed over the singer's decision to write all the songs on her third album, *My December*.

big-game hook—and it's a huge leap forward for the entertainer as a more confident, ever-maturing vocalist."[41]

The title track from the album became another highly popular single. "Breakaway" was written by alternative rock star Avril Lavigne. Clarkson explained on her website why she chose to record it: "I could relate to that song. It describes how I got into the business, verbatim. I did grow up in a small town, I wanted to get out, I felt like there was something … not better for me, but something different for me."[42] Clarkson's version of the song appeared on the soundtrack for the movie *The Princess Diaries 2: Royal Engagement*. She also sang "Breakaway" and "Since U Been Gone" during her time as the musical guest on *Saturday Night Live*.

The other number-one hit to emerge from *Breakaway* was "Because of You," a song Clarkson wrote about her family. The song discusses Clarkson's parents' divorce from her perspective, reflecting that the trials her family went through when she was growing up made it difficult for her to trust people later in life. Fans connected with the emotions in the song, and it quickly became one of Clarkson's most notable songs.

Clarkson's big hit single "Breakaway" was used on the soundtrack for *Princess Diaries 2: Royal Engagement*.

Addicted (to the) Tour

With four chart-topping singles, *Breakaway* sold over 6 million copies to become the third-highest-selling album of 2005. The album's success meant that Clarkson found herself in constant demand to sing her hit songs in public. She accepted invitations to appear in televised concerts surrounding the

Clarkson found that over the course of the Addicted Tour, the feel of her songs changed from being strictly pop to having a rock edge.

NFL Super Bowl and NBA All-Star Game. Clarkson also launched a concert tour in the summer of 2005 to support the album.

In an effort to improve her live performance skills, Clarkson arranged for her Addicted Tour to play at smaller theaters across the country instead of at huge stadiums. During the tour, Clarkson found that she enjoyed performing her songs live and connecting with audiences. "I love it," she noted. "I think it's a cool thing for the fans to get to know you better, hear your music, and see you as a performer and not just a writer or singer."[43] The upbeat, rock-based sound of *Breakaway* proved to be perfect for a concert setting. "I want my music to have just a lot of life—to where people want to get up and jump around," Clarkson declared. "That's the concert I want to have. People let loose and don't care what's going on. They're not worried about work, they're not worried if they've had a bad time with their girlfriend or wife or husband. They're just having fun."[44]

Grammys and Gratitude

The success of *Breakaway* not only translated into hit songs and a popular concert tour, but it also helped establish Clarkson as one of the leading artists in the American music industry. Her work received a great deal of recognition, including a 2005 People's Choice Award for Best Female Recording Artist and back-to-back MTV Video Music Awards for Best Female

Love and Friendship

Early in her career, Clarkson referred to herself as "very old-school, conservative in [her] thinking when it comes to relationships." She said, "Love is something you work at. It doesn't come easily. There are going to be bad days. You are going to have to work at loving someone when they're being an idiot. People think they're just going to meet the perfect guy. Don't be ridiculous."[1]

At the time, she indicated that marriage was not something she was particularly worried about, instead placing the highest value on the friendships she maintained. When she did eventually get married, it was to long-time friend Brandon Blackstock. The couple were married on October 20, 2013. As of 2019, they have four children: two, from Blackstock's earlier marriage, and two together.

1. Quoted in Allison Glock, "Rebel Yell," *Elle*, July 2007, p. 156.

Though she did not date much as a young woman, Clarkson fell hard for her now-husband Brandon Blackstock (far right), and they were married in 2013.

Video (for "Since U Been Gone" in 2005 and "Because of You" in 2006).

Clarkson also won two prestigious Grammy Awards in 2006. *Breakaway* was honored as the Best Pop Vocal Album of the year, while "Since U Been Gone" was recognized as the Best Female Pop Vocal Performance. When she received her awards, Clarkson gave two lengthy, tearful acceptance speeches. Although she thanked her friends and family, as

The Grammy wins were important for Clarkson, proving she was more than just a flash in the pan.

well as many other people who had contributed to her success, Clarkson did not mention *American Idol*. In interviews later, Simon Fuller claimed that he felt no resentment toward the singer. "I'm extremely proud that Kelly won two Grammys for this album," he stated. "No one deserves it more than her. As our first winner, Kelly will always be a big part of the *American Idol* legacy."[45]

Remaining True to Her Roots

Clarkson's two Grammy Awards for *Breakaway* confirmed her status as one of the best artists on the American music scene. Clarkson's popularity continued in 2006, even though she released only one new single, "Walk Away." Clarkson was the most-played artist on American radio for the year and had at least one song ranked in the Billboard Top 40 for a record 111 weeks.

Many other young singers and musicians who have reached similar levels of fame have struggled with their new celebrity status. Clarkson, however, stayed remarkably down-to-earth. Instead of turning into a demanding diva, she remained friendly, outgoing, and accessible. Simon Fuller argued that Clarkson's personality played an important role in her appeal to fans. "I can't think of anyone who sings better than Kelly Clarkson," he said. "She is the best young singer in the world right now. She is a global superstar. And fans really identify with her, because of her openness. You feel like she is a friend, that you know her. That sets her apart."[46]

Even though Clarkson had gained fame and fortune, she seemed determined to live her life the same way she did before *American Idol*. She hung out with the same group of friends, enjoyed the same pastimes, and wore the same casual clothing. In fact, Clarkson did not seem to mind being photographed with messy hair and no makeup. She knew that if she allowed herself to get swept up in the madness of fame and celebrity, she could lose touch with what had made her successful in the first place: her down-to-earth personality.

"It's Good for People to See Normal"

Since she first came to public attention on *American Idol*, Kelly Clarkson has often been mentioned as a positive influence on young women because she projects a healthy body image. There is enormous pressure on women, and particularly women in the public eye, to maintain extremely thin figures. They are able to do this through long hours of training and expensive nutrition plans, something not everyone can afford or has time for, setting an unrealistic standard. Clarkson has tried to be a model for young women to see that all body shapes are beautiful and to embrace yourself as you are.

At one time, however, Clarkson struggled with issues of weight and self-acceptance. As a freshman in high school, she lost a part in a musical to a less talented girl who was thinner and more attractive.

At that impressionable age, Clarkson concluded that she had to lose weight if she hoped to be successful. "The lesson I took from that was purely superficial," she recalled. "It wasn't smart. I headed straight into an eating disorder and became bulimic for the next six months." Eating disorders are extremely common among young women and can be fatal if untreated. With the support of friends, Clarkson was able to overcome her disorder, and ever since has been a vocal advocate for body positivity. "I'm definitely thicker than most people in the industry, but not in real life," she has pointed out. "I think it's good for people to see normal."[1]

1. "Kelly Clarkson's Bulimic Past," ET Online, June 22, 2007, www.etonline.com/celebrities/spotlight/48684.

Instead of getting caught up in the trappings of fame, Clarkson kept her focus on the music itself. She said, "I've always just wanted to sing and write."[47] Unlike many other pop stars, Clarkson also largely succeeded in keeping her private life out of the tabloids. She never partied at nightclubs, for example, and she avoided dating anyone in the spotlight. All in all, Clarkson behaved like a normal person rather than a pampered celebrity. "She appears free of ego or crippling insecurity. She is a normal dress size. She smiles," noted one interviewer. "She is, no caveats, a pop star you can feel good about liking."[48]

Making Her Music Her Own

The graceful manner in which Clarkson handled her fame made her popular with fans as well as many people within the recording industry. As it turned out, Clarkson would need all of that support and goodwill when she became involved in a high-profile battle with her record company.

The troubles began when Clarkson went to work on her third album, *My December*, in 2006. She hoped to build upon the success of *Breakaway* by creating an album that was even more representative of her musical style and interests. For Clarkson, this meant writing all the songs that would appear on the album. "Clarkson wanted her next album to be more personal, to reflect her experiences and sensibilities, and she decided not to work with the professional songwriters and producers who had previously supplied her with infectious anthems,"[49] one reviewer explained.

When *Breakaway* producer Clive Davis learned of Clarkson's plans, however, he expressed doubts about putting out an album made up entirely of her own songs. "Kelly has shown writing ability, and I think she's probably going to want to try her hand at writing all her material in the future," he acknowledged. "I don't want to dismiss it, I'm rooting for her, but we'll see."[50]

Clarkson expected to face some doubts from Davis and other RCA executives. After all, *Breakaway* had earned so much money for the label that she felt certain they would want to follow the same formula in the hope of repeating its success. However, Clarkson also believed that the enormous sales of her previous album put her in a strong position to try something new and to express herself artistically. "My resistance upsets a lot of people, because we could make a lot of money. And I'm not hatin' on money," she explained. "I'm just not comfortable doing things that don't feel like me."[51]

In the end, Clarkson decided to follow her instincts and put together the kind of album she wanted. "There's always this battle, and it's not a bad battle to have. I mean, you obviously don't want 'yes' people around you. And [Davis] and others at the label have been in the business far longer than I have. So obviously you take their opinions in," she noted. "Ultimately, though, I always go with my gut. My gut has done pretty well for me, so I don't see why I shouldn't keep listening to it."[52]

Clarkson was candid in interviews about the struggles she had with her producers. It was an openness that was refreshing for many interviewers and for the public, who loved her down-to-earth personality.

The Battle Begins

Clarkson knew that she was going to have to fight to make the album she wanted and that there was a lot of risk involved in making that album, but the experience of making her first two albums gave her the confidence to pursue the creative growth she wanted to achieve. The same confidence that had served her before would serve her now. She knew she had talent and that creative risks were part of artistic growth, so she planted her feet and got ready to stand her ground.

Chapter Five

Her Own Woman

By this time, Clarkson had two extremely successful albums under her belt. She was a Grammy Award–winning artist and had more than proved herself to her post-*Idol* doubters. Despite these artistic victories, Clarkson found herself facing an ongoing struggle to take full creative control over her work. Part of this meant fighting to write all the songs for her third album, to be titled *My December*. Although they had granted her a large degree of involvement in the writing process for *Breakaway*, RCA Records blanched when Clarkson said she wanted full control on her third outing. Their disagreement over the album's content was heavily publicized by the media in the spring of 2007, leading to some uncertainty about Clarkson's future.

Risks and Rewards

Clarkson's life had changed wildly since she released *Thankful*, and she wanted to use *My December* to explore some of her experiences and emotions since her career had catapulted her into the public eye. To that end, she replaced Davis as the executive producer on the album and insisted on writing or co-writing all of the songs on the album.

As *My December* began to come together, it became clear that most of the songs Clarkson wrote had a darker, angrier feel than her previous work. Her lyrics were more complicated than before, and her melodies moved further away from pop and toward an edgier rock sound. Although Clarkson realized that these changes might make the new album less popular than *Breakaway*, she was willing to take that risk in order to express herself as an artist. "Some of the songs are not what 10-year-olds are probably going to listen to," she acknowledged. "This record is more intense, it's more raw, it's more emotional... Even if it does tank, who cares? It's one album! Out of a whole career of albums I'm going to have."[53]

Although Clarkson claimed that she did not care whether *My December* sold well, Clive Davis wanted to release an album that would be commercially successful. When the RCA Records chief heard the songs that Clarkson had selected for the album, he became very upset. He complained that

Clarkson may not have been as worried as her producers about the sales of *My December,* but she gamely went on a promotional tour to promote the album.

the album was too negative in tone and lacked an obvious, radio-friendly hit. In fact, Davis was so concerned about the tone of the album that he reportedly offered Clarkson $10 million to drop five of her original songs and replace them with others of his choosing. Clarkson, however, insisted that she was happy with the album and refused to make significant changes to it. "If I were to make 'Breakaway II,' I would have failed myself," she explained. "I don't mind [failing], as long as it is my decision."[54]

"Women Can't Possibly Be Good at Two Things"

Arguments over the content of *My December* delayed the release of the album for several months. During that time, both Davis and Clarkson discussed the situation publicly and spoke to the media about their views. The singer argued that her past successes should allow her to make her own decisions about the future direction of her career. She claimed that sexist attitudes prevented recording executives from taking her seriously. "I've sold more than 15 million records worldwide, and still nobody listens to what I have to say," she stated. "Because I'm 25 and I'm a woman."[55]

Clarkson recognized that her youth and gender played into RCA's hesitance to release an album that contained only her own songs. Although she had shown good instincts in her song selection and creative direction, the prevailing attitude was that she did not know enough about her fans or the music market to be trusted with her own music. In other words, they did not trust that she could sing and write. "I'm a good singer, so I can't possibly be a good writer. Women can't possibly be good at two things," she said of the record label's attitude. This did not stop Clarkson from forging ahead on her own path anyway. "I haven't lost my temper about it. It only drives me more. If your thing is to bring me down, cool. I'll just work harder."[56]

Clarkson's vision for her third album was one that reflected where she was creatively and emotionally, as a person and an artist, but RCA wanted to create an album that would reflect popular tastes at the time to maximize sales. The fight would come down to a fundamental difference in approach.

An Uphill Battle

Davis's view seemed to ring true when in April 2007, RCA released the first single from *My December*. "Never Again"—an angry, pounding rock song about a bad breakup with a boyfriend—initially made it into the Billboard Top 10. It received limited radio airplay, however, and dropped quickly down the charts.

Though Clarkson had won the fight for creative control over the content of *My December*, the mediocre performance of "Never Again" and the slow sales were worrying, both for Clarkson and RCA. Though Clarkson had always taken the long view, understanding that she would have some successful albums and some that flopped, there was enormous pressure for her to continue churning out hits.

By the time *My December* was finally released on June 26, 2007, the album had been at the center of a storm of controversy for several months. "The buildup has been nothing short of astonishing," noted one reviewer, "as the blogs, newspapers, magazines, and TV shows have pounced on every fresh development."[57]

When they actually listened to Clarkson's work, however, a number of critics had to admit that the whole situation had been blown out of proportion. They generally agreed that *My December* was not the terrible, amateur album that media coverage had led many people to expect, though it was admittedly not of the same consistently high quality as *Breakaway*. "The original American Idol is fighting a good fight, one that will likely help her career in the long run," wrote one critic. "Unfortunately, *My December* isn't as good as her intentions. Not only will it not match the popularity of *Breakaway*, which featured a string of hits, but it's not as artistically sure-footed."[58]

A longtime idol of Clarkson's, Reba McEntire would become a mentor, good friend, and eventually even her mother-in-law.

The main criticism of *My December* was that it did not make full use of Clarkson's voice, though many made an exception for the last song on the album, "Irvine," which showcased Clarkson's voice alongside an acoustic guitar. Describing "Irvine" as "a timeless song of deep longing," a *Hartford Courant* critic wrote that Clarkson "sings sweetly in a low, dusky tone that is heart-stopping. It's a far cry from the manufactured pop of, say, 'Miss Independent,' and it's the unmistakable sound of an artist pushing herself to grow."[59]

The album also sold significantly better than the disappointing performance of "Never Again" had led people to believe it would: It debuted at number two on the Billboard 200 chart and was certified platinum. Eventually, it would sell over 2.5 million copies. Because the *My December* tour had been canceled, Clarkson instead partnered with Reba McEntire on a series of performances and duets, including a country version of "Because of You," which ended up becoming the lead single for McEntire's album *Reba: Duets*. Throughout the following year, McEntire and Clarkson joined forces for the 2 Worlds 2 Voices Tour, which acted as the official album tour for both *Reba: Duets* and *My December*.

Art as a Mechanism for Growth

Although the content of *My December* received mixed reviews, Clarkson's determination to make an album on her own terms earned her the respect of many critics. Several analysts pointed out that it was unfair to judge the value of the singer's work just by the level of commercial success it achieved. After all, some of the best music often appeals only to a small group of people. In addition, unsuccessful albums have been an important step in the career development of many great musicians. "For an artist to grow over a creative

My December was Clarkson's least successful album in some ways, but it was arguably the most important of her career.

lifetime," explained a critic for the *Los Angeles Times*, "she needs to take side roads and make mistakes."[60]

Even though the results of her efforts on *My December* were uneven, many people felt that Clarkson deserved praise for developing her artistic style. "Kelly Clarkson is much too talented to make an awful record. So when she veers off course … it's forgivable and even encouraged—if only as a swift learning lesson in her blossoming career," one reviewer stated. "With *My December*, Kelly Clarkson has proven she has the courage … to helm what is undoubtedly going to be a golden career."[61]

Regardless of *My December*'s sales performance, Clarkson had won two victories by standing her ground. First, she had taken creative control of her career, and although that meant any failures would be her own, so, too, would the successes. Second, by standing up to those who doubted her, the singer showed courage and integrity that would help her develop as a mature, independent artist worthy of respect. "Kelly Clarkson has proven to be a strong and independent 'good girl' for women to look up to in this industry," said author and self-esteem expert Jessica Weiner. "She was the first big winner of *American Idol* and I think she could have gone in a lot of different directions, but she's really stayed true to herself, and you can see it."[62]

No longer under the shadow of *Idol*, Clarkson had made a name for herself at last as a singer, songwriter, and artist.

In Search of a Cohesive Sound

Clarkson learned a lot from her battle over *My December*, both about the music business and about what she wanted out of her career. She had been prepared for the album to be a flop, but it was not—it sold well and was not nearly the disaster Davis and RCA had feared. In 2009, Clarkson released *All I Ever Wanted*, which debuted at number one on the Billboard 200 chart and was nominated for Best Pop Vocal Album at the Grammys that year. Clarkson wrote roughly half of the tracks on the album and collaborated with several new producers to find a sound that could stay true to her vision while

More to Life than Music

Time and time again, Clarkson has been praised for her extraordinary voice, her energy in performances, and her genuine personality. More than just a musician, she has been a vocal advocate for equality, body positivity, and respect in the workplace. She has spoken out against sexism in the music industry and volunteers with Musicians on Call, an organization that facilitates music performances for hospital patients. Clarkson has also supported causes like HIV/AIDS charities, Save the Children, and UNICEF. In addition, for a while, Clarkson maintained an animal sanctuary in Texas. She has partnered with organizations to promote fair trade and early childhood education, and she has helped provide food for underserved children. In 2014, alongside Reba McEntire, Trisha Yearwood, and Garth Brooks, Clarkson raised more than $400,000 for Tennessee charities.

Philanthropy and advocacy is important to Clarkson—she sees her fame as a platform for her to be able to speak out about her beliefs and a platform she feels she has a duty to use. "It's weird, but I actually came with a brain, not just vocal cords, and it would be silly to not have an opinion," she said in an interview with the *New York Times*. "It would be a disgrace if I didn't have an opinion. It would be a cruel irony to all these people who live in different countries who don't have an opinion, and don't count, for me not to take full advantage of all the opportunities that are laid before us here in this nation."[1]

1. Caryn Ganz, "Kelly Clarkson Is Nobody's Puppet," *New York Times*, October 19, 2017.

growing a little more accessible for the pop charts. Critics, however, were mixed on the album; despite its successful singles, many felt the album of a whole failed to come together as a cohesive project.

Hugh Montgomery of the *Guardian* wrote that the album "is musically conservative, lyrically hackneyed, yet blessed with cast-iron tunes … taken on its own limited terms, it's a job well done."[63] Elsewhere, critics cited Clarkson's extraordinary voice and well-chosen vocals but wondered when she would pull together the tour-de-force album she was capable of. "Like everyone else, she rises and falls on the strength of her tunes," mused Jody Rosen in her review for *Rolling Stone*. "She has made brilliant singles, and may yet record a great album."[64]

If *My December* was her first swing at creative independence, *All I Ever Wanted* represented Clarkson's attempt to strike a balance between commercial success and artistic fulfillment. As she had always done, Clarkson used her experience as an opportunity to learn and grow, and in 2011, she released her fifth studio album, *Stronger*, which would finally bring together all the differing sounds and influences that Clarkson loved—and it would win her another Grammy.

"One of Music's Most Remarkable Voices"

RCA Records released Kelly Clarkson's *Stronger* on October 21, 2011. The album had thirteen tracks, of which Clarkson again co-wrote about half. The album moved away from the high levels of production that had been a source of criticism on *All I Ever Wanted* and instead attempted to emulate the experience of seeing Clarkson live. The album made a cohesive sound out of the different genres that Clarkson loved. In her review of the album, Jody Rosen wrote,

> *Kelly Clarkson's fifth studio album is based on a simple formula: 1) Put Clarkson in a room with a microphone; 2) Give her a solid pop song to sing; 3) Get … out of the way. It's a*

Although *All I Ever Wanted* was a return to a more mainstream sound, Clarkson had won the bigger battle by having more control over the content of the album than she had on *Thankful* and *Breakaway*.

sound strategy. … Stronger is as deft as any Clarkson album, with 13 catchy songs that hover between pop rock, R&B and Nashville – all of them showcases for one of music's most remarkable voices.[65]

Stronger debuted at number two on the Billboard 200 chart, was certified platinum, and received four Grammy nominations. Of the nominations—for Best Pop Vocal Album, Record of the Year, Song of the Year, and Best Pop Solo Performance—she took home Best Pop Vocal Album.

In many ways, *Stronger* marked a turning point for Clarkson. Her next three albums would build on its success: First, 2013's *Wrapped in Red* made Clarkson the first female artist to have the best-selling holiday album of the year; then, 2015's *Piece by Piece* marked the end of her contract with RCA and earned three Grammy nominations; and finally, in 2017, Clarkson released *Meaning of Life* with Atlantic Records, which won her a record fifth Grammy Award nomination for Best Pop Vocal Album alongside a nomination for Best Pop Solo Performance. The sound was a departure in the sense that, with her new label, Clarkson felt she was able to finally make an album over which she had complete creative freedom.

A profile in the *New York Times* reflected that *Meaning of Life* showcased Clarkson "fully happy with herself, personally, professionally, her music. … [P]eople have always not only just loved her voice, her music, but her."[66] By staying true to herself and her vision, Clarkson has been able to achieve for herself what she always wanted: a career with staying power.

A Long Career—and Getting Longer

In recent years, Clarkson has begun to branch out from music. She has written children's books inspired by her daughter, River Rose, which include titles like *River Rose and the Magical Lullaby* and *River Rose and the Magical Christmas*. Each book is paired with an original song, written and performed by Clarkson.

Stronger was another key album for Clarkson and one for which she won a Grammy in 2013.

She also joined the *Idol*-like talent search *The Voice* in 2018 as a coach and judge, alongside Alicia Keys, Adam Levine, and Blake Shelton. She won her first season, the first new coach to win—no surprise, given her history with this type of competition.

In May 2019, the film *UglyDolls* was released. In it, Clarkson voiced a character named Moxy and also contributed to the soundtrack. It was also announced that Clarkson would host her own daytime talk show beginning in fall 2019.

Clarkson was the first coach to win her first season on *The Voice*.

The past five years have been, for Clarkson, an opportunity to explore not just who she is but who she wants to become. As she experiments with her talents in other arenas—books, movies, and talk shows—it strengthens the core that has been a part of her music forever. Since the day she walked onto *American Idol,* it has been clear: "She's been the same genuine, super-talented person she's been from the beginning."[67]

Notes

Introduction: Kelly Clarkson: Pioneer

1. Quoted in Howard Cohen, "Miss Independent," *Miami Herald*, June 30, 2006.
2. Quoted in Ed Bark, "Idol Winner Keeps Up Hectic Pace, But Really, She Just Wants to Sing," *Dallas Morning News*, June 9, 2003.
3. Quoted in Allison Glock, "Rebel Yell," *Elle*, July 2007, p. 156.

Chapter One: Small-Town Girl, Big-Time Dreams

4. Quoted in Douglas Perry, "American Idle," *Fort Worth Star-Telegram*, March 2, 2003.
5. Quoted in Perry, "American Idle."
6. Quoted in Barry Koltnow, "She Enjoys the Moment: Kelly Clarkson Feasts on the Fruits of Winning *American Idol*," *Orange County Register*, June 18, 2003.
7. Quoted in Skip Hollandsworth, "Since She's Been Gone," *Texas Monthly*, May 2005, p. 150.
8. Quoted in Josh Tyrangiel "Miss Independent," *TIME,* February 13, 2006, p. 68.

Chapter Two: America's First Idol

9. Quoted in Bud Kennedy, "Kelly Clarkson Getting By with a Little Help from Her Friends," *Fort Worth Star-Telegram*, September 27, 2002.
10. Quoted in Tyrangiel "Miss Independent."
11. Simon Cowell, *I Don't Mean to Be Rude, But….* New York, NY: Broadway Books, 2003.
12. Quoted in "Kelly Clarkson," *Biography Today*, vol. 12. Detroit, MI: Omnigraphics, 2003.
13. Quoted in Tom Gliatto, "On with the Showdown!" *People*, September 9, 2002, p. 52.

14. Quoted in Mark Brown, "Just Thankful: Clarkson Happy She Did Things Her Way on TV Show, CD," *Rocky Mountain News*, April 12, 2004, p. D8.

15. Andrew Marton, "*American Idol* Winner Has Warmth and Charm to Spare," *Fort Worth Star-Telegram*, September 4, 2002.

16. Quoted in "Kelly Clarkson," *Biography Today*.

17. Brill Bundy, "Live on Tape: In the Audience for *American Idol*," Zap2It.com (via Knight-Ridder/Tribune News Service), August 14, 2002.

18. Bundy, "Live on Tape: In the Audience for *American Idol*."

19. Quoted in Skip Hollandsworth, "Since She's Been Gone," p. 150.

Chapter Three: The Struggles of Success

20. Quoted in Lynette Holloway, "Act Two," *New York Times*, October 14, 2002, p. C9.

21. Jeff Leeds, "Idol Winners Try Stretching Out Their Fame," *New York Times*, November 3, 2004, p. E1.

22. Quoted in "Kelly Clarkson," *Biography Today*.

23. Quoted in Brown, "Just Thankful."

24. Quoted in Perry, "American Idle."

25. Quoted in Hollandsworth, "Since She's Been Gone."

26. Quoted in Perry, "American Idle."

27. Quoted in "Kelly Clarkson," *Biography Today*.

28. Quoted in Brown, "Just Thankful."

29. Quoted in Ron Martinez, "Clarkson Having a Fair Old Time," *Milwaukee Journal-Sentinel*, August 6, 2003.

30. Quoted in Jon Bream, "Beyond 15 Minutes," *Minneapolis StarTribune*, June 15, 2003.

31. Quoted in Tyrangiel, "Miss Independent."

32. Henry Goldblatt, "Win Beneath Her Wings," *Entertainment Weekly*, April 25, 2003, p. 149.

33. Quoted in Tyrangiel, "Miss Independent."

34. Stephen Holden, "Cotton Candy Effigies and a Best Friend from Hell," *New York Times*, June 21, 2003, p. B13.

Chapter Four: Taking a Risk

35. Quoted in Glock, "Rebel Yell," p. 156.

36. Quoted in S. Tia Brown, "Success Stories," *Teen People*, March 1, 2006, p. 64.

37. Quoted in Gary Graff, "No False Idol," *Cleveland Plain Dealer*, April 8, 2005, p. 4.

38. Quoted in Graff, "No False Idol."

39. Quoted in Tyrangiel, "Miss Independent."

40. Natalie Nichols, "Clarkson Breaks from 'Idol' Spotlight," *Baltimore Sun*, December 30, 2004. www.baltimoresun.com/news/bs-xpm-2004-12-30-0412290135-story.html.

41. Chuck Taylor, "Kelly Clarkson: Since U Been Gone," *Billboard*, November 20, 2004, p. 67.

42. Quoted in "Breakaway Bio," KellyClarkson.com. www.kellyclarkson.com.

43. Quoted in Don Thrasher, "What Could Have Been a Reality-Show Novelty, Kelly Clarkson Turned into a Real Pop Music Career," *Dayton Daily News*, August 14, 2005, p. F1.

44. David Burke, "Pop Goes the Idol," *Wisconsin State Journal*, August 6, 2003, p. D1.

45. Quoted in "Idol Not Her Idol?," *Cincinnati Post*, February 10, 2006, p. C10.

46. Quoted in Glock, "Rebel Yell."

47. Quoted in Glock, "Rebel Yell."

48. Glock, "Rebel Yell."

49. Joan Anderman, "Her Independent Step Went a Little Too Far," *Boston Globe*, June 19, 2007.

50. Quoted in Tyrangiel, "Miss Independent."

51. Quoted in Glock, "Rebel Yell."

52. Quoted in "Kelly Clarkson Nixes Tour over Slow Ticket Sales," CNN, June 15, 2007.

Chapter Five: Her Own Woman

53. Quoted in Anderman, "Her Independent Step Went a Little Too Far."

54. Quoted in Glock, "Rebel Yell."

55. Quoted in Glock, "Rebel Yell."

56. Quoted in Glock, "Rebel Yell."

57. Preston Jones, "Kelly Clarkson's Third Album Is Littered with Seething Heartbreak," *Fort Worth Star-Telegram*, June 26, 2007.

58. Glenn Gamboa, "Kelly Clarkson's New CD *My December*," *Newsday*, June 26, 2007.

59. Eric R. Danton, "Clarkson's New Album, Though Uneven, Shows Growth," *Hartford Courant*, June 26, 2007. www.courant.com/news/connecticut/hc-xpm-2007-06-26-0706260864-story.html.

60. Ann Powers, "Kelly Clarkson's Dispute with Clive Davis Has Made Her Music Hard to Hear," *Los Angeles Times*, June 26, 2007.

61. Brendan Butler, "Kelly Clarkson's *My December*," CB Music, June 25, 2007. www.cinemablend.com/music.

62. Quoted in "Lessons for Bad Girls," *Showbiz Tonight*, CNN, June 12, 2007.

63. Hugh Montgomery, "Kelly Clarkson: All I Ever Wanted," *Guardian*, March 7, 2009. www.theguardian.com/music/2009/mar/07/kelly-clarkson-all-i-ever-wanted.

64. Jody Rosen, "All I Ever Wanted," *Rolling Stone*, March 3, 2003. www.rollingstone.com/music/music-album-reviews/all-i-ever-wanted-190340/.

65. Jody Rosen, "Stronger," *Rolling Stone*, October 25, 2011. www.rollingstone.com/music/music-album-reviews/stronger-191512/.

66. Caryn Ganz, "Kelly Clarkson Is Nobody's Puppet," *New York Times*, October 19, 2017. www.nytimes.com/2017/10/19/arts/music/kelly-clarkson-meaning-of-life-interview.html.

67. Ganz, "Kelly Clarkson Is Nobody's Puppet."

Kelly Clarkson Year by Year

1982

Kelly Brianne Clarkson is born on April 24 in Fort Worth, Texas.

1988

Clarkson's parents divorce, dividing her family and forcing her to become more self-reliant.

1995

A junior high music teacher hears Clarkson singing in the hallway and invites the seventh-grader to join the school choir. After her solo at a school assembly receives a standing ovation, Clarkson sets her sights on becoming a professional singer.

2001

Clarkson moves to Los Angeles in hopes of breaking into the music industry, but she is forced to return home to Texas four months later when her apartment is destroyed by fire.

2002

At the urging of a friend, Clarkson tries out for the reality-TV singing competition *American Idol*. Her strong voice and engaging personality help her advance to the finals, where she defeats rival Justin Guarini to win a million-dollar recording contract.

2003

After several delays, Clarkson releases her first album, *Thankful*, in April. By the end of the year, it sells a respectable two million copies to be certified double platinum by the Recording Industry Association of America. Clarkson also co-stars in a movie with Justin Guarini, *From Justin to Kelly*, and finishes second in the inaugural *World Idol* singing competition.

2004

Clarkson releases her second album, *Breakaway*, which features several of her own compositions. Its harder-edged, rock-oriented sound distances her from *American Idol* and earns her critical acclaim and two Grammy Awards.

2005

Clarkson is a featured performer during telecasts of the NFL Super Bowl and the NBA All-Star Game. She also appears as a musical guest on *Saturday Night Live*.

2006

Clarkson is the most-played artist on American radio for the year.

2007

Following a highly publicized battle with Clive Davis and RCA Records over her decision to write all of her own material, Clarkson releases her long-awaited third album, *My December*.

2009

Clarkson releases *All I Ever Wanted*, which earns her another Grammy nomination for Best Pop Vocal Album.

2011

Stronger, Clarkson's fifth studio album, is released and wins her a Grammy for Best Pop Vocal Album.

2013

Clarkson's *Wrapped in Red* Christmas album becomes the first by a female artist to be the best-selling holiday album of the year.

2015

The last record that Clarkson would make with RCA, *Piece by Piece*, is released.

2016

Clarkson's first album with Atlantic Records, *Meaning of Life*, earns her Grammy nominations for Best Pop Vocal Album and Best Pop Solo Performance.

2018

Clarkson joins another vocal talent show, *The Voice*, but this time, as a judge. She is the first coach to win in her first season.

2019

UglyDolls, a film in which Clarkson sings and plays a character named Moxy, is released, and in the fall, her daytime talk show debuts.

For More Information

Books

Contemporary Musicians, vol. 73. Detroit, MI: Thomson Gale, 2012.

This reference chronicles Clarkson's musical career through the release of her fifth studio album, *Stronger*.

Grohl, Virginia Hanlon. *From Cradle to Stage: Stories from the Mothers Who Rocked and Raised Rock Stars*. Berkeley, CA: Seal Press, 2017.

This unique book looks at music stars from a different perspective: their mothers! Clarkson's mother discusses her daughter's musical formation in this book.

Tieck, Sarah. *Kelly Clarkson: Original American Idol*. Edina, MN: ABDO Publishers, 2014.

This book describes Clarkson's historic victory on *American Idol* and how she coped with the sudden fame that came after it, up through her holiday smash, *Wrapped in Red*.

Websites

American Idol
(www.abc.go.com/shows/american-idol).
American Idol began airing on ABC in 2018. The official website for the ABC TV program features highlights of each season, information on contestants, news updates, photos, and other information for fans.

Kelly Clarkson
(www.kellyclarkson.com).
Clarkson's official website offers a biography, news updates, tour dates, and links to sources of more information.

Kelly Clarkson on Instagram
(www.instagram.com/kellyclarkson).
Clarkson's personal Instagram provides fans with photos and commentary from her career, family, and personal life.

Kelly Clarkson on Twitter
(twitter.com/kellyclarkson).
Clarkson's official Twitter account is the perfect place to find updates on her career and to get insight into her daily life.

Index

Y

Picture Credits

Cover Kathy Hutchins/Shutterstock.com; pp. 8, 12–13, 23 Kevin Winter/Getty Images; p. 11 Jean-Paul Aussenard/WireImage/Getty Images; p. 18 Fairfax Media/Fairfax Media via Getty Images; pp. 20–21 Jon Soohoo/WireImage/Getty Images; pp. 24–25, 34–35 SGranitz/WireImage/Getty Images; pp. 28–29 Kevin Winter/ImageDirect/FOX/Getty Images; p. 39 Kevin Winter/ImageDirect/Getty Images; p. 41 Michael Ochs Archives/Getty Images; pp. 45, 57 Theo Wargo/WireImage for Clear Channel Entertainment/Getty Images; p. 47 L. Cohen/WireImage/Getty Images; pp. 50–51 Dimitrios Kambouris/WireImage/Getty Images; p. 53 Yui Mok - PA Images/PA Images via Getty Images; pp. 60–61 Lee Celano/WireImage/Getty Images; pp. 62–63 Rodrigo Varela/WireImage/Getty Images; p. 65 Steve Granitz/WireImage/Getty Images; p. 66 Dan MacMedan/WireImage for The Recording Academy/Getty Images; pp. 70–71 L. Busacca/WireImage for XM Satellite Radio/Getty Images; pp. 74–75 George Pimentel/WireImage/Getty Images; pp. 78–79 Joey Foley/FilmMagic/Getty Images; p. 80 C Flanigan/FilmMagic/Getty Images; p. 84 Dr. Billy Ingram/WireImage/Getty Images; p. 86 Kevork Djansezian/Getty Images; p. 87 Tara Ziemba/Getty Images for NBC.

About the Author

Edna McPhee wanted to be an astronaut when she grew up, but when NASA stopped sending people to the moon, she decided to become a writer instead. She has written for a variety of different publications as a journalist and short-story writer. She currently lives in the mountains of Colorado with her two dogs, named Tom and Jerry, and an entire room filled with knitting yarn. She still wants to go to the moon.